Divinely Flawed

and

Wildly Amused

Newsflash: Life is hard—pretty much in equal measure for all of us at one point or another, and we all need a leg up sometimes if we are to "embrace the suck" with any amount of grace. While it's true that we are all part of the same cosmic whole, it is imperative that each of us do our best to be whole as individuals before evolving together. How many times have you wished that life came with a guide book, some little set of instructions to get you through the day? Well, here you go!

Perhaps you've been on an airplane where the overly cheery flight attendant has announced, "In the unlikely event of a drop in cabin pressure, oxygen masks will magically drop out of the overhead compartment. Please put the oxygen mask on yourself first and then on your child." "Wait, what?… Um, no" It is most parents' instinct to give that lifesaving breath to their child first, right? But think about it (Ms. Cheerypants reminds you); if you're unconscious, how will you save your child? This book is inspired by the idea that before you can be of service to, or in relationship with, anybody else, you have to turn in and connect deeply with yourself. Think of this book as your spiritual oxygen mask; by spending moments a day with the tiny reminders herein, may you live a more peaceful, balanced life and show up in the world as the best possible version of yourself.

Divinely Flawed

and

Wildly Amused

Little Contemplations For A Big Life

Amanda Freed LMT, RYT, CMT
Edited by Nicole DeHaven Calhoun

Divinely Flawed and Wildly Amused: Little Contemplations for a Big Life

Published by Gatekeeper Press
3971 Hoover Rd. Suite 77
Columbus, OH 43123-2839
www.GatekeeperPress.com

ISBN: 9781619847583
eISBN: 9781619847576

Printed in the United States of America

Welcome, Dear Friends
Allow me to introduce myself and my offering:

In my professional life, I've been blessed to enjoy a long history of serving humans. I've worked as a hair stylist, yoga instructor, meditation teacher, massage therapist, and energy healer. In many of the aforementioned capacities, I felt much like the proverbial bartender, listening to peoples' stories, their headaches, heartaches, hopes, and dreams…and yeah, they wanted advice. I was seventeen at the beginning of this journey; who was I to offer guidance?

I longed to gain more wisdom in order to serve as many people as I could. I studied every bit of yogic philosophy I could and learned from the best. In my many yoga teacher trainings, I was taught to weave an intention or theme into the postures that would not only expand the physical experience but imbue the students with a feeling, inspiration or spiritual lesson. In those trainings, I was taught how to carefully distill huge concepts into a sentence or sometimes a phrase, a teaching skill for which I'm forever grateful. As I now teach yoga and meditation, I find that these insights have become the reason many show up to class 3-4 times a week and have kept coming for over 15 years, and now I'm honored to share a sampling of them with you.

Wildly Amused

I hope you are wildly amused by your mistakes
and enamored of your imperfections. I hope you
are in love with the person you are. The universe
has created each of its beings as divinely flawed.

Familiar Zone

Fear of growth creates the shackles of comfort that are strangling you. Only when you become willing to move from your familiar zone will you know the magnitude of your magnificence.

Worrier vs. Warrior

Are you a worrier or a warrior? Worry is a lack of faith in the future, in the universe, in oneself, or in another. A worrier sets his/her sights on future disasters that may or may not occur. A warrior has faith in his/her own power, embracing the present moment and taking action.

Indecision

Indecision is a clever ruse of the mind. You grapple with the folly of this or that, here or there, do or don't. The spirit is led not by the mind but by a wisdom teacher inside you that knows the desire in your own heart. Look not to the periphery for what is clear at the core.

Truth

Telling your truth with compassion at all times
can only result in the highest outcome for
all involved. There is no other possibility.

Divine Vehicle

Your body is the earthly vehicle for expressing yourself as the divine in this lifetime. You are an embodied, sentient being, and as such, your first job is to honor and care for your vehicle. Any attempt at spirituality is secondary.

Your Story

You are not your story. You are not where you've been, whom you've known, or what has happened to you. You are not the choices you've made, your job, hobbies, or family of origin. You are an expression of divine perfection with a spirit that is constant and consistent. You are a manifestation of love, bliss, and light.

Your Show

You are the main character, the producer, and the director of your show in this lifetime. You wrote the screenplay, built the set, hired the actors, and created the dialogue. Every scene has been orchestrated by you for your evolution. All parties involved have agreed to be involved for their higher learning as well.

Weighty Words

People talk because they have mouths. Do not fault others for what they say; instead, assess the weightiness you place on their words.

Just You

There is nobody else in the room; others show up as mirror images. "You are mistreating me" translates to "I am mistreating myself or allowing myself to be mistreated." We are simply reflections of one another and can choose to acknowledge the other as an illumination of self.

Who's Holding What?

Emotions themselves are inanimate, and as such, they don't have the ability to hold you; you hold them. Although they are real and valid, they reside on the surface layers of your being, and therefore cannot threaten the deepest level of your consciousness.

Holding Space

To hold space for another or oneself without trying to change or improve the current situation is to offer deep love and full acceptance. The highest gift you can offer is your presence and ability to stand in what is. Rough waters will subside, the storm will pass, and the threshold will have been crossed with your love as a port in the storm.

Vantage Points

The earthly classroom offers an upwardly
spiraling curriculum. As one climbs the
ladder of consciousness, he/she arrives at
increasingly higher vantage points. Each trial
is a lesson, a step up onto the next rung. Floor
seats at the game provide a limited view;
allow yourself to change perspectives.

Balance

Balance is a dynamic process: imperfect,
unstable, ever in flux and flow. If you'll
allow yourself to get off course just a bit, to
invite a bit of a fall, the spirit will right itself.
Honor the waverings along the way.

Energy

Energy cannot be destroyed, but it is finite. It is the currency in the bank of your being. How long until you empty your energetic account? How will you refill your coffers?

I Don't Know

To say, "I don't know" is to offer a gift of wisdom and empathy; in doing so, you empower others to creatively solve their own problems while acknowledging your own imperfection and vulnerability.

Darkness

Do not fear your shadow side. Be willing to delve within and pierce through the depths of your own darkness; at the other side lies your light.

Shhhh...

Language can never sufficiently convey ideas or emotions. Speak less, say more…count and consider your words carefully. Your quiet, powerful presence - or absence - speaks volumes.

Making Space

You determine your worth by deciding
what to keep in your life. By releasing that
which is no longer serving your highest
good, you automatically make space
for a finer set of circumstances.

Where Ya Livin'?

Everything on the planet is vibrating within a certain frequency. You only have the ability to interact with that which matches your current vibratory rate. Lower your frequency and limit your choices; raise your vibration and the possibilities are endless.

Which Voice?

The voice of spirit is never angry, judgmental or punitive; it is always compassionate, kind and loving. Remember this when trying to discern whether the source of your inner dialogue is spirit or the "chatterer."

Stop Chasing Happiness

Genuine happiness doesn't lie in gratitude or platitudes; it cannot be found through romance, busyness, or other external pursuits. It's already yours, though hidden at times. Trust that there is a wellspring of bliss that resides in perpetuity deep within.